FACTORS INFLUENCE TRAVELER AND STUDENT PSYCHOLOGY

JOHN LOK

Contents

Preface

Introduction

This book divides two parts, first part explains what factors can raise student learning interest and second part explains what factors can raise traveller travelling entertainment interest. I discover that education service and travelling service both industries have similar factors to persuade students to raise interest to learn and travellers to raise travelling entertainment interest. Also, these factors will influence their learning or travelling entertainment psychology to bring positive learning or travelling entertainment behaviours in order to carry on travelling entertainment to the country or learning need to the school persuasively. I shall explain what factors can influence them to do learning or travelling behaviors attractively.

This first part, I shall indicate education industry how and why can apply behavioral economic method raise student individual interest to learn. I shall indicate these several aspects to explain the reasons. They include how to apply behavioral economic methods to solve classroom management discipline in order to let student individual to raise learning interest in the classroom; how successful persuasive teaching method can raise student individual learning behavior ; how effective school management behavior can raise student learning interest and how to improve financial education effectiveness which can raise student learning interest. However, I shall indicate evidences to explain how and why above these methods can persuade students to change their learning attitude to feel more interest to learn in schools. This book is suitable to teachers and educational psychologists and educational researching students to study.

Nowadays, global travelling entertainment activities are popular. Some travellers like domestic travelling or some travellers like to catc airplanes to go to other countries travel. In consumer behavioral view point, when the consumer discovers the product's price is higher than the another product's price. Then, he/she will usually to choose to buy the cheaper product, such as travel agent travelling entertainment activities arrangement service case, whether the travelling provider charges higher travelling entertainment activities arrangement service fee to compare the another similar travelling entertainment activities arrangement service provider. Does this travelling entertainment activities similar fee comparison factor influence any travellers choose to find the cheaper travelling entertainment activities arrangement provider? If travelling entertainment activities arrangement price is not the main factor to influence traveller individual choice. What other factors can influence traveller individual travelling entertainment activities arrangement choice? I shall explain what the other factors are influcenced traveller individual travelling entertainment arrangement choice.

The factors include that the cultural distance on satisfaction and travel intention factor, the lifestyle concept in travel behavioral factor, the business travellers motivation behavioral factor, the impacts of peer-to-peer accommodation use on travel patterns factor, factors influence local tourists decision-making be on choosing a destination factor, transportation, shopping centers, travelling destination facilities supplying factor, social media travelling networking sites promotion factor, traveller's travelling experience psychological factor, travelling service for disabled people's travelling need factor, green travel entertainment service for environment protection travelling environment need factor the impact of travel blogging on the tourist, traveller individual vacation destination choice factor, economic impact to the traveller individual sudden changing factor.

Therefore, it brings these questions: How any why traveller individual travelling choice won't be influenced by travelling entertainment service price only? Does it mean the travelling entertainment service providers will not reduce their traveller number when they can respect or consider above factors to avoid to bring negative influence to traveller consumers, but they still change higher travelling entertainment arrangement service fee to them?

The second part , such as travel entertainment industry, nowadays global travelling entertainment activities are popular, some travellers like domestic travelling or some travellers like to catch airplanes to go to other countries travel. In consumer behavioral view point, when the consumer discovers the product's price is higher than the another product's price. Then, he/she will usually to choose to buy the cheaper product, such as travel agent travelling entertainment activities arrangement service case, whether the travelling provider charges higher travelling entertainment activities arrangement service fee to compare the another similar travelling entertainment activities arrangement service provider. Does this travelling entertainment activities similar fee comparison factor influence any travellers choose to find the cheaper travelling entertainment activities arrangement provider? If travelling entertainment activities arrangement price is not the main factor to influence traveller individual choice. What other factors can influence traveller individual travelling entertainment activities arrangement choice? I shall explain what the other factors are influenced traveller individual travelling entertainment arrangement choice.

The factors include that the cultural distance on satisfaction and travel intention factor, the lifestyle concept in travel behavioral factor, the business travellers motivation behavioral factor, the impacts of peer-to-peer accommodation use on travel patterns factor, factors influence local tourists decision-making be on choosing a destination factor, transportation, shopping centers, travelling destination facilities supplying factor, social media travelling networking sites promotion factor, traveller's travelling experience psychological factor, travelling service for disabled people's travelling need factor, green travel entertainment service for environment protection travelling environment need factor the impact of travel blogging on the tourist, traveller individual vacation destination choice factor, economic impact to the traveller individual sudden changing factor.

Therefore, it brings these questions: How any why traveller individual travelling choice won't be influenced by travelling entertainment service price only? Does it mean the travelling entertainment service providers will not reduce their traveller number when they can respect or consider above factors to avoid to bring negative influence to traveller consumers, but they still change higher travelling entertainment arrangement service fee to them? In my this part, I shall explain above factors how to influence traveller individual behavior to let readers can predict traveller individual behavior more accurately.

Prologue

Table of content

CHAPTER ONE

Behavioral economic solves classroom management discipline

How to apply behavioral economic method to help teachers to solve classroom management discipline in order to raise student individual learning interest in classrooms? Students need to know what classroom management means. It means effective discipline, it is being prepared to motivate students to raise interesting to learn in classrooms. It is providing a safe, comfortable learning environment, it can build the teacher individual student's sale esteem and creative and imaginative in daily lessons.

Why has classroom management relationship to student individual behavior as well as why behavioral economic method can be applied to solve classroom management discipline in possible? It is simple because every teacher teaching styles, personality attitudes and every teacher management strategies are different and are not effective. It is possible that due to teaching experiences. Student population to every lesson, low or high salary level, every teacher individual time preparation and time management factors. Then all issues concern whether every teacher to do choice to arrange whose time to prepare before he/she will teach which lesson on that day. For example, if the teacher feels tried to teach more than fine lessons on that day, because he/she is sick. But the school has no enough teachers number to replace the student to teach his/her students on that day. So, he/her teaching performance can not b better , satisfaction and enjoyment in teaching are dependent upon how he/she leads students to cooperate.

Hence, he/she can not permit to so personal rest behavioral choice, and he/she feels that salary can not be raised to double payment or more to get overtime allowance on that teaching day. It will bring any unsatisfactory and unenjoyable teaching attitude or poor teaching behavior or performance and teacher won't deal with discruptive behaviors. Buy, also manage to minimize off task, non-disruptive teaching behavior to teach students and manage their own behavior to learn in classroom effectively and efficiently. Their poor classroom management behavior will bring poor teaching performance. Hence, students won't feel the school teachers are good teachers and students' families will lose confidence to let the school teachers to teach their students.

In Behavioral economic teaching method view point, the school needs to review whether its teachers number is enough to prepare some teachers need to rest at home suddenly. So, other teachers can replace them to teach any his/her lessons on that day immediately. If the school neglected to employ extra enough part time teachers number to prepare to replace any full time teachers who have need to rest on any days. Due to salary expenditure increasing reason, it is not good choice to reduce to employ extra part time teachers number to avoid the sudden full time teachers number shortage need. It will bring classroom management changes poor, due to unsatisfactory teachers' teaching need to go to classroom to teach their students in classrooms when they are sickness on that teaching day suddenly. Therefore, poor teaching performance or poor classroom management behaviors to the teacher which will bring poor economic loss, e.g. student enrollment number reduces, students absent number to every lesson increases school teaching subjects number decreases too the school in long time.

Therefore, all these poor influences will cause the school's economic loss, it is due to the school teachers' teaching behaviors are poor , due to many teachers do not enjoy and feel satisfactory to teach these students and manage classes disciplines effectively. It seems that whether the school has enough teachers number, it can influence how teacher individual teaching and class management behavior to be better or worse and then which will have relationship to influence the school's economic gain or loss in long term consequently.

Therefore, in teacher individual behavioral psychological view point, every one ought have effective time allocation method to prepare how to teach whose students in every lesson. I shall recommend how the teacher individual behavioral economic choice to solve discipline challenges in classrooms as below:

1. Transitions vs. allocated time method
The school teachers can allocate time periods they intend for their students to be engaged in learning activities as well as they can arrange transition time allocated for learning activities. For example, getting students assembled and attentive, assigning reading and directing to begin, getting students' attention away from reading and preparing for class discussion in their schools.

The transition is allocated time to teacher individual behavioral goal is to increase the variety of learning activities , but to decrease transition time, student engagement and non-task behaviors are dependent on how smoothly and efficiently to teachers more from one learning activity to another.

Therefore, teacher has witness if when classroom discipline problems occur, the teacher consistently takes action to solve the misbehavior of exactly those students who do in classrooms, when two discipline problems arise as the same time, the teacher can deal with the more serious first. The teacher can decisively handle instances of off- task behavior before the behaviors either set out of hand or are modeled by others. When handling misbehavior makes sure all students learn what is unacceptable about that behavior, deal with misbehavior without disrupting the learning activity.

2. Classroom rules for student individual behavioral conduct. Formalized statements that provide students with general guidelines for the types of behaviors that are require and the types that are prohibited a few rules are easier to remember than many rules, each rule in a small set of rules is more important than each rule in a large set of rules.

Why do need necessary classroom rules of conduct? It aims to maximize on -task behaviors and minimize off-task (discuptive) behaviors, secures the safety and comfort of the learning environment, prevents the activities of the class from disturbing other classes, establish an learning environment in which achieving specified learning goals takes priority over other concerns in classrooms, be particularly prepared and organized to minimize transition time and utilizes a communication style that establishing non-threatening, comfortable environment to let students to learn in classrooms. Other components of disclosure statement include: basis course outline, grading procedures, include procedures for making up missed work, extra credit homework expected etc., attendance policies should be consistent with school policy, other class rules, policies procedures, safety considerations as necessary , accommodation for disabilities statement, signature of student and parent / guardian. Therefore, classroom rules can influence how student individual chooses to do whose learning conduct or behavior , even improving their learning attitude in classrooms. Classroom rules are the best method to influence every student how to choose to do whose learning behaviors in classroom in order to earn the most effective learning benefits for themselves.

Finally, I shall discuss how to apply behavioral economic method to raise student learning interest at classrooms? As I explained that when teacher feels that individual satisfactory or enjoyable teaching feeling to do his/her teaching job, which will influence whose teaching performance in classrooms. Thus, how to improve every teacher individual teaching performance or method or teaching quality which will be important factor to influence whose student individual learning interest to be raised in classrooms indirectly.

I recommend that teachers need to concern how to arrange classroom teaching environment to be attractive or safe or enjoyable to influence every student individual learning attitude to increase more attention or concentrate to hear whose teacher's teaching to his/her any lessons in the classroom more considerately. Arrangement is determined by learning activity (lecture, class discussion, small group work etc. learning activities in classrooms). Thinking thorough class procedure and learning activities and arrangement the classroom in the best possible way.

Teachers need to know why the student chooses to do his/her behavior in classroom. Usually, every behavior has a function , three primary reasons for disputive behavior in the classroom include power, attention, what to be left alone (i.e. disinterest or feelings of inadequacy). Many misbehavior are exhibited by students are responses to a behavior needs exhibited by the teacher to understand why a person exhibits behavior is no reason to tolerate it, teacher needs to understand the function of a behavior will help in knowing how to deal with that behavior. When, the teacher can understand why the student chooses to do his/her behavior to find the solutions to persuade or dissuade the student does not choose to do the harmful behavior or change the harmful behavior to do right behavior in order to influence other students can not concentrate on learning considerately.

Consequently, if the school expected to raise every student individual learning interest in classrooms. The school needs to find methods to let its teachers feel satisfactory to teach their students in the school as well as the school's teachers need to learn how to understand why the student chooses to do harmful behavior to influence other students concentrate on easier learning in an enjoyable learning classroom environment.

When the school can let its teachers to enjoy to do their teaching jobs and they can feel more satisfactory when they are teaching every time in classroom as well as its teachers can understand some students why they choose to do harmful learning behavior to influence the other students to concentrate on learning in classrooms and they can find the solvable methods to dissuade they do not choose to do harmful learning behavior to influence other students can not concentrate on learning in classrooms again. Then, between the school's teachers and students both can build positive teaching attitudes and learning attitudes in order to cause they can choose to do enjoyable and satisfactory teaching behaviors or performances to teacher and concentration on learning behavior or attitudes to students in classrooms.

Consequently, when the school can build a good classroom learning environment to let teachers consider to teach their students in order to bring whose students can concentrate on learning in classrooms. Then, a good classroom learning environment will bring good learning economic and non-economic benefit , such as student number increases , school income increases and teachers salaries increase, student individual attention will raise, student will enjoy to go to school and absence number will reduce. Consequently, any schools' teacher individual teaching behavior and student individual learning behavior both in classrooms which must have positive or negative relationship to bring the school itself and the teachers themselves long term economic and non-economic benefits in learning behavioral economic view point. Also, the importance is that learning behavioral economic analysis, can explain why the teacher individual good or bad emotion can influence his/her every lesson student individual learning emotion to be good or bad to do learning behavior in clasaroom. So, schools need to concern every teacher individual emotion whether he/she feels enjoyable or satisfactory to teach his/her students in classrooms in order to avoid every classroom students' learning emotion will be influenced to be poor to bring long time economic loss to the school. It is one important factor to influence any school's teaching performance to be succeed.

CHAPTER TWO

Successful persuasive teaching method can raise student individual learning behavior

Can teachers apply behavioral economic method to raise student individual learning behavior? Behavioral economic method is explained by psychology and other disciplines to create models of limits on rationality, willpower and self-interest. Although, economic professionals believe it can be applied to predict consumer behavior. But, how any why can it be applied to raise student personal interest to learn new knowledge in education industry aspect? This is one valuable research question. If it can be applied to educational psychology aspect to raise student individual learning interesting influentially, educators ought need to learn to how to do in order to persuade student individual has more interest to learn in anywhere schools or homes or libraries in habitually persuasively. I shall explain some possible educational psychological methods as below:

When one student discovered that learning will bring much tangible and intangible benefits to influence his/her career development in the future. For example, he/she can find good jobs, earn more salaries, raise the high class social positon, build personal successful image or raise satisfactory feeling, raise social competitive effort in job market etc. different economic related benefits or non economic related benefits both. Then, the teacher or the school will have possible to persuade whose students to raise learning interest when they choose to learn in the school.

How to let the student to feel the school can give good economic related or non-economic related benefits to satisfy the student future career plan successful development need persuasively and attractively? It will need to include psychological factor to influence its students to raise learning interest when they are studying in the school in whose learning experience stage. I assume that every student will learn hardly when the school can persuade its students can believe that they must earn good career benefit when they can follow the school's discipline to learn hardly in whose whole learning stage in the school.

Therefore, one successful persuasive teaching method can influence or persuade the students choose to learn hardly . Usually, in general students need not expect to waste learning time and money to chose one poor teaching quality of school to study. If they can not achieve good examination results or they need increase long time to extend their graduation time, then they will feel waste money and time loss to choose the wrong or unsuitable school to study. It is one rational either positive or negative learning feeling when one student gain good or bad examination result consequently.

Hence, one successful school must let students to have confidence , it can raise good quality teaching method to let them to study as well as it can provide good learning environment to let them to feel safe, enjoyable , attractive , persuasive learning attitude when they go to school to enter the classroom to learn every day. So, the school must need to let all students to feel they won't waste money and time economic or non-economic related losses when they choose the school to learn, if the school expected to persuade its students to choose to learn easily.

Therefore, learning behavioral economic theory explains that student individual learning interest whether whose interest is raised or not which has been related to influence whether he/she feels his/her learning attitude or learning behavior will bring either waste learning time and money loss or not in whole learning career in the school consequently. Usually, every student won't expect to waste his/her learning time and money if he/she can not earn economic or non-economic related benefits to his/her future job career.

It implies that non-wasted time and money psychological factor brings to the student feeling to learn that will be one man economic factor to influence the student chooses to do hard learning behavior. For example, when a young age student does not choose to go to the school, because he/she does not concern whether he/she will earn a better life in the future.

He/she must be persuaded to feel the school is fun now or is given no better opinion to compare the school. Hence, the school needs to let the young age student to feel there are not other schools opinions are better to compare to the school as well as the school can provide attractive teaching method to let the student to feel more fun to learn when he/she chooses the school to learn.

Therefore, providing fun learning environment and fun teaching method both factors will be one important to encourage the student to learn hardly. The particular educational outcomes worth encouragement, such as attainment, attendance, and homework issues of these educational components will must be achieved fun learning feeling to let the student to whose learning interest encouragingly or persuasively. So, fun learning environment can bring the student individual learning interest in possible. It means that if the student does not feel fun to learn when he/she goes to the school to learn every day. Then, he/her poor fun learning feeling will discourage he/she feels why he/she needs to go to school to attend every lesson to learn in classrooms hardly. So, fun learning environment. fun teaching method, fun homework, fun learning content etc. teaching related components factor will encourage every student likes to go to school to listen every lesson hardly every day in possible.

Present-biased learning behavior has important implications in education. Doing fun home works, studying for fun exams, researching fun colleges or potential opportunities for financial aid and completing applications all involve educational cost which will let any students choose to weigh the future learning cost to evaluate which school will be possible to bring educational loss spending cost to evaluate whether he/she ought to choose which school to study in preference. Hence, it explains that the student will consider whether the school can provide fun learning environment and fun learning subjects or courses to let them to choose to study and whether he/she can feel fun teaching method to satisfy whose learning need. Then, the school will be possible increased successfully chance to let the student to choose it to enroll to study in preference. Moreover, attractive courses choices, providing fun learning environment, providing good and fun teaching method quality , fun teaching book contents choices to let students to study etc. these factors will encourage students to raise learning interest successfully.

However, any schools need focus only on salient factors , it implies that even simple optimizing decisions may not always be made. So, with a better understanding of student individual fun learning environment and fun teaching method learning need and fun courses teaching learning contents , subjects choices etc. these factors will possible bring knowledge to design more effective learning policies and improve student individual learning outcomes.

Moreover, improving student learning attitude factor is also important to raise whose learning interest. For example, by reading motivational passages or watching movies which can encourage students to focus on positive identifies related to learning and intellectual curiosity may be one approach a growing evidence suggests that many students and parents are not fully informed about education costs , future economic and non-economic related benefits and options. It is possible related to whose low-income family backgrounds and poor learning attitude both factors. So, if the family was one high income family, it will have possible to influence whose sons or daughter to build good learning attitude. When they have good learning attitude and good family growing relationship . The, they will raise learning interest , due to they had built from good learning attitude when they are living in one good family relationship environment. In special, when the family is one low income family and low educational level background, parents will been to work, so they will neglect to teach whose sons or daughters to know whether they ought how to learn easily, which will be one correct or right learning attitude to learn by themselves successfully. They will neglect and lack useful educational recommendation to compare education cost, future economic and non-economic educational benefits and learning attitude and opinion methods and the suitable courses and teaching books contents opinions to let whose their sons and/or daughters to know how to learn effectively by themselves, instead of school teaching method. So, these students' parents' lacking useful learning recommendation or negligent education learning recommendation behaviors which will also cause the low income family students to build " discouraged hard learning attitude" to let them to raise interest to learn any more new knowledge persuasively. Even, due to the non-educational behavioral opinion of pre-school decision making opinion, if the parents discovered that the school is one suitable school to let their sons and/or daughters to learn persuasively or attractively in order to let they can earn good examination results or pass subjects more easily. Then, these disappointed parents and low grade examination result of students will feel need to learn more hardly if they are still not improving their grade when they feel that they had been studying hardly in the school. Consequently, it will bring more negative learning emotion to the students and families. Hence, disappointing or poor or negative learning attitude or emotion to the student's feeling , this factor must not raise the student individual interest to learn in the school. Otherwise, positive or good learning emotion or attitude will influence the student to raise learning interest to continue to learn in the school consequently. hence, schools ought not neglect to improve students to build positive learning emotion or attitude habitually in order to raise whose interest to learn in the school more easily.

CHAPTER THREE

Can effective school management behavior raise student learning interest

How and why effective school management behavior can influence the school's student individual to raise learning interest. What is the relationship to bring student individual learning interest to be raised between the student and the school? An effective school management behavior can make the function bring that teaching and learning take place in the most effective way. In managing school's systems have to operate so that a whole range of social, intellectual and emotional activities can evolve and develop (pay foot et , 1989). It seems that an effective school management system can change student individual to do a range of positive social, intellectual and emotion activities in order to raise whose learning interest.

Therefore, innovating the traditional education system, changing many aspects of school structures, systems and organization as well as recognizing that the more teachers at all levels in a school's hierarchy who had management training of some kind, the better is needed to some traditional educational organizations. Any educational organizations need have good management functions ,which include: setting the right aims and objectives, planning how a goal will be achieved, organizing available educational resources (how teaching time arrangement, how to select teachers and clerical staffs, homework, how revision time allocation, how educational material opinions, e.g. computers facilities, classrooms number and design method and teaching environment, lecture hall seats number, tables and chairs number, library teaching book lending supplies number etc. resources arrangement) . Therefore, the school can be economically achieved in a planned way, controlling the teaching process (i.e. ensuring that the goal is achieved, e.g. raising learning interest to every individual student when he/she is learning at classrooms, reducing the students fail exam and/or test result number.

In fact, if the school expects it can be one real teaching organization, if the school can arrange internal and external structures effectively. Then, the school let students to have more confidence to choose the school to study. Internal structures include: class organizing, subject choice organization, departments organizing, responsibility arranging. Otherwise , external structures include: admission numbers, numbers on raising salary scales, school budget, leaving ages, holiday length of the school day, arrangement methods of appraisal etc. Hence effective school management system can bring more confidence to the student to choose to the school to study and it can encourage him/her to raise learning interest effectively.

So, it seems that student learning interest has close relationship to concern how the school manages its organization. Because good school management can influence its internal and external teaching resources how to allocate to use and manage effectively. For example, good classroom teaching environment can influence students to feel easily, an teaching book library can have enough different topic teaching book to let students to borrow to read, or it has enough commuter facilities to let students to find any reading data from internet conveniently. Then , they will be influenced to raise learning interest more easily, because the school has one attractive and fun learning environment to let its students to learn.

Therefore, an effective school management system can influence its students to raise more interest to learn in order to influence they choose to do learning behavior to study more harder in homes or schools. How to bring one effective school management system to influence students to feel? I shall indicate the main factors as below:

The first factor is one effective school management system needs have an effective hierarchy of head teachers, deputy heads, heads of department different effective organizing systems. It aims to achieve more directing, controlling and commanding to any department leaders to manage themselves departments more easily.

One educational organization's hierarchical pyramid can indicate such as: a head teacher manage or leads one deputy or more than one deputies on the top level, the middle level will include one deputy or more than one deputy manager(s) or lead(s) in one department head or more than one department heads. Next, the middle level will include one department head or leads more than one teacher at the low level. However, any school organization expects to manage or lead themselves schools effectively. They need to organize in such a way that they will try to achieve effective results and make every effort to maintain good relationships between those who work in these departments.

Consequently, when the school can have effective hierarchical structure to manage all different teaching staffs to do whose individual teaching behavior effectively. Then, it will bring positive emotion influence to every teacher to teach whose students more effectively. Hence, every classroom students' learning attitude will enjoy to bring more learning feeling when they are real raised learning interest from their teachers' teaching method influence persuasively.

The second factor is that each staff group participation. It will be the school's staff group participation behavioral factor, how it influences every classroom overall students' learning behaviors to be positive learning emotion or attitude when they (every classroom overall students) are listening their every teacher individual teaching in every lesson in every the classroom. It is important to find out who participates a lot and why, as well as why someone, e.g. teacher contributes every little to the classroom students. For example, it is because of fear, disagreement or disinterest, the group of teachers may under have useful point to make. So, a group should ideally encourage all its participates to contribute to any discussions and decision making. This issue of participation is one that group leaders have to consider very carefully.

In fact, influence and participation to every teaching group are not always the same. Some teaching staffs who tell a lot may not always be listen to . Others who are quiet and speak very little can, when they do speak, capture, the attention of everyone. If this is the case then whoever participates may alter and change depending on who has influence at a specific time and who needs certain individuals to speak and support his or her particular cause.

The final factor is that the school needs to know how the styles to be influenced to every teaching group. Influence can take may forms, it can be both positive and negative. It can either to support or co-operation of others or refuse or nor support or co-operation of others. How this happen with a teaching group can be autocratic teaching colleagues who will attempt to impose their will on the teaching group by movement towards directions in which they eagerly support everyone and everything and try to avoid conflict at any cost and those who is influenced by distancing themselves from the whose proceeding influence others to do the same. Hence, in a effective teaching group , the teacher's header, e.g. deputy or head teacher ,the middle level staffs or the top level staffs will need to manage themselves every teaching group, e.g. each classroom teacher individual teaching behavior is more easily and effectively. When the classroom teacher can have good teaching performance to teach his/her students in the lesson. Then, he/she can raise every lesson's student individual learning interest more easily or persuasively.

The final school management factor is that, what is the most suitable or right school ethos and whose school aims to the school. If the school chose the most right school aims, then it can able to develop attitudes which won't only help pupils to learn more effectively or raise their interest to learn only, even , it can shoe them the technique of learning and how to continue to want to learn. I shall recommendation that these characteristics of the most suitable or right school aims in order to achieve effectiveness and a positive ethos the following characteristics will help as below:

An effective and powerful leadership, the deputy head needs to be involved in all major decisions, all teachers need to feel that they own those decisions that directly affect them, there to be consistency and continuity throughout the school organization, e.g. in terms of discipline, patterns, homework number and course content test or examination questions contents allocation policies, resource management, subject courses timetable structures etc. teaching sessions need to be structures, matched to pupils' needs, the actual teaching should be intellectually challenging for all pupils, the learning environment of the school whether it will be task -and -work orientated, i.e. every pupil will recognize learning is the norm rather than the exception, there will be lots of communication between teachers and pupils both inside and outside the classroom, record-keeping and assessment are sensible and thorough and are communicated to parents when necessary in a way that they can understand, whether there is a positive learning climate where emphasis is placed on praise rather then criticism control in classrooms is firm , but fair, with children being treated as individuals, any teaching or resource allocation , teaching time allocation activities whether are organized to take place outside the classroom and away from the school. This is a means of offering pupils wider experiences and a way of putting. The academic content of the curriculum into a different content.

Consequently, how to organize the school in effective way factor which will be one main influential factor to influence teachers to do positive or negative teaching behavior to persuade whose students can raise more learning interest in classrooms. So, it seems that teacher individual positive or negative teaching emotion or attitude will influence their teaching performance or teaching behavior to improve to be better in order to raise the school's students' learning interest more easily or persuasively.

CHAPTER FOUR

Improving financial education effectiveness through behavioral economic to raise student individual learning interest

How any why does improve financial education effective behavior which can raise student individual learning interest? How to innovate application of lessons from psychology to a financial education programe which can raise student individual learning interest effectively? I shall apply student learning behavioral economic methods to explain why and how improving finance education can be effective to raise student individual learning interest.

The standard economic approach to financial education argues that financial consumers will behave in their own best interests of the financial market is perfectly competitive. In fact, in education industry, education consumers, e.g. student parents do not have enough all the knowledge and information concerns what where their sons and/or daughters ought need to choose which subject(s) to study which are(is) the most suitable their interest and effort to learn, whether what the school fee budget level is the most reasonable, what the course contents are the most effective to let their sons or/and daughters to learn easily etc. different related educational institutes information questions to have enough time to prepare to gather these information in order to compare which school is the best or the most suitable school choice for their son and/or daughter to study more easily.

Thus, of the student consumer's parents can have enough fully information concerns to education institutions how to assist them to make the most reasonable school choice making decision more accurate. Then, they will have less worry and complain less if they felt the school is not the most suitable school to let their child(children) to study because they had enough data gathering concerns which school individual courses and fee etc. educational related factors comparison before. Then , the education market can function properly. When the student's parents believe that they had found the school, which was the most suitable school to let their child(children) to study. Then, the fully education institutions information can help their children(child) has (have) more confidence to feel to finish the course more easily. However, they will face one challenge of the choice to the most suitable school issue, it needs to change more expensive school tuition fees to their students. But they have no enough money to support their child(child) to study the most suitable school. They must not forgive if they need to choose another school to replace it to study. Because they must believe that this school is the most suitable school to let their child(child) to choose to study, due to they had enough education information to compare which is the most suitable school to let their child(children) to study. Therefore, if the country's government can lend financial education subsidies to assist their children (child) to pay the more expensive school fee to study. Then, when they finish their studying course in the school, even after they can find good job to do to earn income. Then, they can permit to pay back their prior school fee to the government in installment payment method, e.g. one to three years maximum installment school tuition fee payment plan.

I believe the country government's installment financial education subsidies program plan can encourage the feeling financial difficult students who can pay school tuition fee to the more expensive school to learn. It will raise their learning interest, due to they need to pay back all school tuition fee to the government after they graduate and when they can find job to work. They do not want to waste their money and time to extend time to graduate , if they failed some subjects and then they need pay more school tuition to the failed subjects again. Then, they will need to pay more tuition fee to the government after they graduate consequently. Therefore, it seems that government's financial education subsidies tuition lending to univeristy students to learn program which can excite all these tuition fee subsidies assistance students to hard to study in their university learning stage.

Because they do not want to pay higher tuition fee to government if they failed some subject(s), they need to increase tuition fee to finish their degree in the university and it will increase interest to pay to government if their tuition fee increases, due to they fail to pass some subjects in their university learning stage. Hence, government's high tuition fee subsidies are leant to the university student, which will excite to them to raise learning interest to expect to pass all subjects in order to pay the minimum tuition fee to the government after they graduate later.

I shall explain the reasons why government's tuition fee educational subsidies program to university students which can influence them to raise interest to learn in their university learning stage as below:

Behavioral economic in educational subsidies program can be used to influence a number of existing education tuition need services and provisions to help to improve the efficacy of financial education to the feeling education financial diffiicult university students. For example, it can better incorporated within the design of different educational financial courses to lend to the difficult university's financial subsidies assistance need students, in order to improve of education service and relevant education products to any universities, increasing students number to the school or raising student individual different courses or subjects choices of studying or learning behavioral change flooring education and incentive commitment and sustained interest to learning behavior to the financial subsidiaries assistance students. Thus, financial education of government's education subsidiaries assistance to university students plan which is only one of the relevant approaches that can be taken to help people to avoid of unwanted psychological traits, when they lack enough money to choose the most suitable university to enroll. So, they only choose to study the another cheaper tuition fee schools to enroll them to study, if their government had not education tuition installment payment assistance subsidies program to lend to them to pay immediately.

Thus, to choose the most suitable university to study. All of these education tuition fee assistance which can influence them often to go to the school in order to attend any lessons to listen their teachers' teaching courses attentively in classrooms. Why do they have interest to go to all lessons to listen their teachers' teaching courses persuasively? Because their attractive learning behaviors are influenced or encouraged or excited by government's education tuition subsidiary assistance program. They do not expect to fail to pass any one of subjects in order to pay extra higher educational tuition fee subsidy to their government later.

Behavioral economics and economic psychology can help to explain the shortcomings of traditional approaches to financial education. But more importantly, they can be employed in the design of more effective educational programs. Education product course design and delivery can also be improved by applying the lessons of behavioral economics. Behavioral economic assumes that students will respond to certain situations , such as lacking enough money to pay tuition fee to study the most right choice university or incentives in predictable ways, such as government supports financial education assistance to the feeling financial difficulties' university students.

It is important that government financial education subsidy to university students policies that draw on the lessons from behavioral economics do not disadvantage student individuals disadvantage student individuals or group of same age students who do not behave in the predicted ways. Although, behavioral economic has not provided to universities with a clear understanding of the link between student individual knowledge and learning behavior, but it does help to explain why the student individual knowledge in itself may not be enough to change the student individual learning behavior easily.

Mechanisms that conclude behavioral economics to change student learning behavior are not absolute acceptable easily. In some countries education policy makers prefer to encourage educational financial assistance lending behaviors to university students through highly student personalized approaches rather than approaches that provide just not only some solution to every feeling financial difficult university students. Their countries believe that there are other better solutions to the feeling financial difficult university students , which can persuade them or encourage them to raise individual interest to learn in universities or high schools more easily than education financial assistance lending solution.

Can behavioral economic be used to make financial education to university or high school students more effective? The actual impact of various financial education institution program choices or subjects on knowledge different financial assistance lending choice program on raising university or high school student individual learning knowledge and raising university or high school student individual learning interest and learning behavior has only recently began studied.

Consequently, any education tuition subsidiary assistance program is as a project or service (or a related collection and services) that is needed systematically structured with the intention of meeting specific financial education goals in order to achieve raising or encouraging university or high school student individual learning interest to any university or high school subject choices aspect successfully. However, the country government's financial education tuition subsidy to university or high school student program whether it can achieve to persuade or encourage the country's university or high school students to raise learning interest to learn in the university or high school student individual learning stage successfully. However, it will have other factors to influence the university or high school student individual choice to study which high school or university in preference, instead of government 's educational financial tuition subsidy plan. But, I believe that government's educational financial tuition subsidy plan which can influence student individual prefers to choose the more expensive universities or high schools to study , because they have educational financial tuition subsidy to assist them to choose the preferable suitable schools to study persuasively, even they are needed to pay higher tuition fees.

Reference

Playfoot, D., Skeltion, M. and Southworth, G. (1989) . the primary school management book. A practical handbook for heads and teachers. London: Many Glasgow.

CHAPTER FIVE

Cultural distance on satisfaction and respect travel intention

Every country cultural difference is different. How and why cultural difference has a real impact on tourist satisfaction and it can also influence to repeat travel. Is cultural tourism one major factor to influence tourist to repeat travelling intention or choice to the country in international tourism choice market? For example, China and India have similar culture. Their cultural difference is not much, e.g. eating cultural habit is similar , entertainment cultural habit is similar. These both countries people do not want to spend much money in eating and entertainment both aspects. Hence, these two countries people do not consider how to consume to enjoy entertainment and eat expensive food. Hence, it is based on cultural similar reason. These both countries tourists will prefer to choose to repeat travelling either China or India. When the Indian tourists had chosen to go to China to travel in the first time. Then, the Indian tourists will choose to go to China to travel in second time again. Also, the Indian tourists had chosen to go to China to travel in first time. Then, the Chinese tourists will choose to go to India to travel in second time again.

What factors influence China and India tourists respect to travel between these both countries. The factors will include cheap air ticket price, cheap hotel living price , less economic cost factor. However, I believe the similar cultural factor will be the major factor to influence many Chinese and Indian tourist prefer to choose to repeat travelling between these both countries.

As my indication to these both countries people have similar eating habits, choosing foods, low health foods, common foods choice eating at cheap restaurant habitual consumption. Also, they have similar entertainment habits, their entertainment demand is not high. They like to ride bicycles to go to anywhere to travel. They like to go to swim, play basketball, football etc. sports. These all sports are cheap sport consumption. So, it based on similar individual low enjoyment demand and low health, food quality demand similar cultural factors. Chinese and Indian people have no long distance cultural difference between eating and entertainment habitual factor will include them to choose to repeat travelling between these both countries. Due to China and India have many restaurants can provide cheap food or sport service providers can provide different kinds of cheap sport entertainment consumption to satisfy their cheap food and cheap entertainment needs in their journey in China or India anywhere. So, it explains that why these both countries tourists will repeat to travel these both countries again after they had visited China or India to travel in first time. So, the similar cultural factor can impact these both countries tourists to repeat to go to these both countries to travel again. Hence, if these two countries‘ cultural distance is far or different, then themselves countries' tourists won't choose to repeat travel between themselves when these two countries for cultural distance tourists had visited to another country in first time. Hence, culture has been continuously considered as a much factor which tourists consider in terms of choice of the destination travelling place. Also, it explains cultural distance which can make tourist individual has less satisfaction to concern to tourists to repeat travels.

Otherwise, for far cultural distance two countries case example, such as Chinese and American , these two countries people's eating habit and entertainment cultural needs are different. For eating habit difference example, American like to eat pork, beefs, chickens, potato to replace rice and other foods. Otherwise, Chinese like to wat rice, vegetables more than potatoes, pork , beefs for lunch , dinner . So , their eating habits are very different. Also, American like to drive boats on the season drive cars to go to anywhere to travel on holidays for sports or holiday entertainment activities . Otherwise, Chinese like to play basketball, football, ride bicycle of cheaper sport entertainment on holidays. So, American entertainment activities are more expensive to compare Chinese. Also, US and China , like families whose power distance is different, such as every per family powerful member is parents, who have more power to give opinions to choose anywhere to travel for whose sons and/or daughters whole family members travelling arrangement.

Therefore, if the Us family powerful members, such as at least one son or/and daughter members who need t choose to go to which country to travel if the family powerful members, such as the child/ children's parent feel China's food taste or entertainment activities are totally different to be similar to their country's food taste and entertainment activities habitually after their whole family members had travelled to China in first time before. Although, their son(s) and daughter(s) will hope to go to China to repeat travel again. But, due to the US family parents are their son(s) and daughter(S) powerful decider to make any travelling decision to choose which country will be next time travelling destination. If their parents feel China's eating and entertainment culture is totally different to their countries. Then, the US family will not choose to repeat travel to the China country again any more easily, because this US family can not feel satisfactory when they visited China in their first time before, due to they feel China 's food and entertainment cultures are totally different to their US country. So, the cultural distance factor will influence the US family don't choose China to go repeat travel again.

Consequently, different countries' similar or different cultural factor will influence the country's tourists choose to repeat travel to the country again. So, any country needs to know what its culture is in order to attract the similar cultural countries tourists to repeat travel to itself country more easily.

CHAPTER SIX

Lifestyle factor influences travel behavior

Whether do different countries tourists‘ different lifestyle which can influence their travel consumption behaviors? Even, which countries that they will choose to go to travel. For example, when one tourist who owns himself/herself often to drive to go to anywhere habitually. The tourist's driving car habital behavior which will influence that he /she will feel need to rent car to travel to anywhere habitually , when he/she selects to go to the country to travel. Hence, if he/she feels the tourism destination has no any rent car service providers to provide him/her to rent any car to travel anywhere in the country's travel destination. Does the country lack rent car service factor which will influence that he/she will still choose to go to the country to travel in preference? For example, when one New Zealander's family who own at least one car at home. So, the New Zealand whole family every member can often drive car to go to anywhere , even, one family member had driven one car to leave his/her home. So, driving own car activity or behavior has been one habitual activity to influence the New Zealand every member to feel the travelling destination needs have rent car service provider supplies cars to let them to rent to travel. The driving car lifestyle has caused the whole New Zealander family driving habit. When the family's sons) and/or daughter(s) need(s) to go to school or go to shopping as well as their parents also need to drive their cars to go to office to work in themselves home town often. In common, there are many New Zealanders who will have at least one car at home because they feel that they can drive their themselves cars to go to anywhere in New Zealand more than waiting bus or tram or train or ferry etc. public transportation tools more conveniently. So, New Zealanders' driving own car habit will influence their lifestyle to feel that they also need to rent cars to travel to go to any where to travel to replace to wait public transportation tools choice in the travelling destination during their journey.

For shopping trips is more influenced by their driving car activities. So, it seems that this New Zealander families will be influenced to their tourism destination need, they need the tourism destination has car renting service provider to be supplied anywhere to let them can drive the renting cars to go to anywhere in tourism destination. It means that when the tourism destination has less rent car providers can provide renting car services to drive anywhere or it has none any renting car service providers are existing in the tourism destination. Then, the renting car service providers number shortage or none any renting car service providers to be provided to the country's tourism destination, which will cause the New Zealander families do not prefer to choose to go to the country to travel generally, e.g. Hong Kong, China, Korea these Asia countries have no many rent car service providers in these countries. So, the New Zealand families won't prefer to choose to go these countries to travel when they discover these Asia countries lack enough rent car service providers to let them to drive to travel in themselves conveniently. Otherwise, America, England, Japan etc. countries have many rent car service providers. So, these countries will be this New Zealander families' preferable tourism countries. Thus, the New Zealand families' driving ownership car lifestyle will influence their travel behaviors to choose to go to the country which can have many rent car providers in the tourism country any where tourism destinations in preference.

Thus, whether the country has renting car service providers , it will be variable factor to influence any country's car ownership families' driving car travel behaviors in their journey in order to let they feel that they can drive themselves ownership cars to go to anywhere to travel conveniently, even when they leave their countries. Hence, these countries' car ownership driving habitual families' behaviors will be influenced their tourism destination or location decision choice when the country has many renting car service providers in preference as well as this renting car service provider supplying factor will be more important to influence the habitual driving own car traveller to be preferable choice to compare other factors, e.g. cheap entertainment consumption providers factor which include cheap hotel living fee, cheap food price consumption etc. expenditure in the travelling country.

Thus, it explains that different countries' car ownership tourists , whose driving own car activities will cause their daily lifestyles, then their daily driving own car lifestyles will influence their tourism destination choices indirectly. So, it seems that lifestyle can be a outcome variable (or dependent variable) factor to influence travel behavior in any travelling built environment. The travelling built environment characteristics can include density measures (population density, job density), job-housing density). These travelling built environment factor can represent what the city resident's lifestyle. For example, where the location in relation to local center or regional center to the country's residents are living. This country resident's living location will cause this country resident's lifestyles , e.g. holiday or leisure whether it is low budget, active and adventurous or frequent traveller with second place or self-organized , family oriented or close to home. Hence, the country's living built environment will influence the country's resident's lifestyles. Due to different countries' residents will have different lifestyles. Hence, built environments and life styles have relationship to influence every country's residents when they need to go to other countries to travel in their holidays. For example, frequent travellers are usually living in big and busy cities, otherwise, non -frequent travellers are usually living in the country sides, where there are less offices or factories are built to let people to work. So, big city will bring busy feeling to the country's residents, then they will be influenced to feel need to often to go to travel for leisure intention in their holidays. Otherwise, countryside will bring not busy or quiet environment feeling to the country's residents, then they won't feel working feeling when they are living in county side. So, they won't feel need to go t o anywhere to travel in their holidays often.

Hence, built environment will bring either busy or not busy (quiet environment feeing) to the both different country residents when they are living in the places. Their living places will cause their lifestyles are different. Then, they will be influences to feel have more frequent travelling needs or less frequent travelling needs to explain why every country people will have more or less frequent travelling needs.

CHAPTER SEVEN

How any why peer-to-peer accommodation can impact business tourism pattern

I shall explain how any why peer-to-peer accommdation can attract business tourisms to choose business tourism intention? Usually , employees or employers buy business trips, why they choose one particular travelling company over another and why the business tourists choose to travel when the peer (more than one business tourists) who will choose to peer-to-per accommodation business tourism pattern more than the more expensive hotel living comfortable feeling business tourism pattern.

Business travel agents need to know or understand what reasons the employer or employee feels peer-to-peer accommodation business tourism motivation is more suitable or better to compare hotel living comfortable feeling business tourism pattern. Why can business tourism accommodation choice factor influence the business tourist's business trip choice.

Business trip means work related travel to an irregular place or work and it represents that one employee or more than on employees business tourists whose expenses are paid by the business ,he or she or they work(s) for. So, in employer's business trip expense view point, he/she expects the employee or employees can choose the most cheap expenses for whose business trip. It also means that the employer does not expect that it is a high quality journey for the employee's or employees' business trip. The business tourism is year-round, peaking in spring and autumn , but still with high levels of activity in the summer and winter months. It may be long time or short time, e.g. less than one month or more than one month, even more than half year for the business trip. When the employee is employees are working permanent full time employment. It is not for leisure intention, it means that the employer does not hope employee or employees spend(s) extra more expense to spend any leisure or goes (go) to any destinations to visit in their/her/his whole business trip.

Hence, it is based on the cheap expenses for the business trip aim, employer usually demands employees or employees to choose the peer-to-peer be cheaper accommodation to live or the employer will help its employee(s) to choose the peer-to-peer cheaper accommodation to live. So, it seems that expensive hotel living facilities won't be the preferable accommodation choice for employer because the business trip pay or reimburse the employee. Hence, business travel agencies ought not help the business tourists to choose expensive travel package, e.g. expensive hotel accommodation on the trip, expensive transportation tools, e.g. taxi renting service to get to business meetings, the cheap peer-to-peer cheap hostel accommodation and cheap transportation tool, e.g. travel buses pre-booking service, or cheap restaurant choice vacation incentives package is more attractive to let them/him/her to choose for their/her/his business trip.

A business person or a peer-to-peer business people also have /her expect to take advantage of frequent flyer schemes which allow him/her/them to take leisure trip with airlines when they/he/she is /are accumulated sufficient miles in the cheap or air ticket(s) to catch air plane for business trip. Hence, he/she /they expect(s) to earn airlines expenses from whose frequent flyer schemes when they/he/she can claim to original air ticket price from whose employer, but in fact, peer-to-peer business tourists or individual business tourist pay lesser air ticket charge from whose frequent flying program accumulated sufficient miles, even no any payment. So, airlines can benefit the business traveller, such as improved in competition millages programs, quick check in and online check in, lounges with broadband connection etc. service.

Why does peer-to-peer accommodation living factor is the most influential to any business tourist(s) to choose the travel agent? In employer's business trip expensive view point, if it has many employees need to go to other countries business trips for long days frequently. Then, the employer will consider whether the every day accommodation living cost is expensive or not. So, comparison hotel and peer-to-peer hotel price, hotel accommodation price is usually higher than small accommodation rent price. When peer-to-peer accommodation has been shown to positively impact to business trip employers in popular. Because any business spending will be one important considerable factor to influence employers to choose. However, the accommodation renting price will be more influential to impact business tourism cost. Hence, employers will estimate every whole business trip expenses how it can impact peer-to-peer or hotel accommodation choice. So, the living budget factor will be one important influential factor to influence any employers how to choose where are the suitable destination for every individual business tourist or peer-to-peer group business tourists to live. So, it seems small size peer-to-peer accommodation are compared to large size expensive hotels more suitable for business tourists.

Although, it is possible that individual employee or a group peer-to-peer employees will feel peer-to-peer accommodation is not more safe than hotel accommodation. But, their/his/her employer usually does not consider safety, comfortable environment issue for their/his/her every business trip. They only consider lose accommodation price issue. So, the accommodation choice will be one critical factor to influence employers how to help their individual employee or a group peer-to-peer employees to choose where he/she/they will live when he/she/they arrive(s) the destination for whose every business trip. Hence, it seems that accommodation will be one critical factor to influence anywhere to be chosen to live for any business trips to their individual employee or group peer-to-peer employees' needs.

7.1 Factors influence local tourists' destination choice

What are the main internal and external factors to influence local tourist's domestic travelling choice behaviors and destination choice decision making? What are the social , cultural , personal psychological factors to influence the decision-making of local tourists to travel to different types of tourism destinations in domestic travelling destinations, e.g. attractions, available amenities, image price external factors. They can influence local tourist's destination choice behaviors. Does the individual occupational reason can influence local tourist's local destination travelling choice? So, any travel agents need to develop and promote of domestic destination need to determine the factors influencing tourist's destination choice.

In a local destination tourist individual productive way, how local tourism agents can bring what factors to influence or charge whose local destination travelling behavioral changes. For example, tourist individual behavior and destination choice factor, the comparison between the current local tourism destinations choice and the past local tourism destinations choice factor. Instead of local different travelling destination prices comparison, journeys comparison . What are the other internal and external factor to influence the local tourist's travelling destinations choices behaviors, e.g. attending local festivals, events, taste local cuisine and be part of unique features of a destination. These will be valuable external or internal factors to influence the local tourist's local destinations choices. So, different countries' local travelling destinations will need have a number of key elements that attract visitors and meet their needs. The key elements may include , for example, primary activities, physical setting and social / cultural attributes primary external activities elements, and secondary elements may include catering and shopping, and addition elements/accessibility and tourists information providing to local tourists.

Due to local destination tourism must be cheaper than overseas or foreign destination tourism. So, the local tourist travel agents need to provide their travelling services to local tourists, more attractions, accessibility , amenities, excellent available packages activities and ancillary services to compare overseas tourism destinations. Because the local tourists will compare the overseas different destinations travelling places to decide whether they ought choose to travel overseas or local different destinations at the moment. So, any entertainment activities concern local destinations which will be local tourists' preferable comparative travelling services to the local travel agent and the overseas travelling service in order to decide whether he/she ought choose local travelling or overseas travelling at the moment.

Hence, local different travelling destinations attractive factor will be one important influential factor to influence local tourist's travelling choices. However, a tourist's attitude, decisions, activities, ideas or travelling experiences evaluating and searching of any tourism service behaviors will influence the final travelling destination choice decision whether he/she ought choose to go to overseas or local travel. He/she will consider how to spend time and money and effort to carry on any kinds of entertainment activities in whose local or overseas journeys. So, the different destination local and overseas internal travelling price and spending entertainment time in journey and spending effort to arranging every travelling entertainment which every will be one considerable issue to compare budget to overseas and local different travelling destinations. If the tourist feel whose country

, e.g. American's local travelling destination budget is spend less than overseas travelling destination too much. Then, the American will choose to local travelling destinations more than overseas travelling destinations and the moment. So, travelling budget will one factor to influence the tourist to choose whether overseas or local travelling.

So, it seems that time, money and effort will be another factor to influence the tourist will be another factor to influence the tourist chooses to go to overseas or local travelling destinations, instead of different travelling entertainment provider choices factor in the local or overseas travelling destinations . Moreover, the tourist's individual income, the local and overseas living condition, formation of cultural and aesthetic tastes, price of local and overseas travelling service and discounts, local and overseas travelling destinations' temperature or weather viable, e.g. number of sunny days, geographical condition, cultural and natural resource, medical tourism etc. external factors will influence the tourist individual final travelling decision to choose either local tourism or overseas tourism entertainment decision.

CHAPTER EIGHT

Tourist individual driving behavior how to impact travel behavior

Does every tourist individual driving behavior influence whose travel behavioral choice? However, individual mobility decisions are possible difficulties for measures aiming at tourist individual travelling behavioral changes and links them to the transport need aspect when the tourist arrives the destination to travel. For example, whether the travelling destination has bus public transportation tool supplies or ferry transportation tool supplies or taxi transportation tool supplied or train or tram etc. different public transportation tools to influence the tourist individual travelling destination choice.

When every country decides to develop travel industry. It needs to understand how to arrange what kind of public transportation tools to be supplied to satisfy any countries‘ tourists mobility needs in whose journeys in order to achieve tourism planning for public transportation system to attract different countries' tourists to choose to arrive itself different destinations to travel more easily. So, the country's transportation services supplies will have permanently impacted to every tourist individual travel behavior towards more mobility when he/she arrives to the country to travel.

Can transportation system factor influence tourist individual travelling destination decision? it depends on the tourist individual attitude or transport needs of decisions. For example, if the city , e.g. New York has many tourists, who are high income, young gender, high education level tourists. Then, they will choose more expensive and comfortable train more than cheap and not comfortable bus transportation tool. So, I assume that the year has many high income, high education , high social class occupation tourists arrive US , New York city . Then, they will choose train more than bus transportation tool to go to anywhere to travel in New York city. So, it is not represent that the city has many cheaper public transportation tool, such as many buses number to be supplied , the bus public transportation tool can bring more income to attract overseas tourists to come to New York travel. It depends on whether the tourist individual characteristics, e.g. high or low income, more or less comfortable transporation tool supplies needs or high or low educational level, alone tourist or family tourist or friend relationship tourist. Any one of these tourist individual psychological factors will influence the tourist to choose either cheap and less comfortable public tool system or expensive and more comfortable public tool system to be supplied to the city to travel. So, the city's comfortable or not comfortable public transportation tool supplies which will influence the overseas tourists how to choose the city to travel.

However, on the tourist's habitual behavior of catching which kind of transportation tools, this factor will bring to influence how to choose the kind of transportation tool(s) whether the city can provide choice to let the overseas tourist to make where travelling decision when he/she arrives to the country. However, his/her transportation tool catching habit will be possible to influence whose travel times for public transport use, instead of which kind of transport tool(s) he/she will choose to catch when he/she arrives the country to travel.

In conclusion, the tourist's age, income, occupation, education level will influence how the tourist's transportation choice in himself/herself country, then it also bring this question: will influence the tourist individual destination choice if the country can provide or can not provide the kind of public transportation tool(s) to let the tourist to choose to catch in his/her journey in the country's city. Hence, it explains that why every country's pubic transporation tool supplies will influence the tourist to choose where to travel in the country.

8.1 What are usually travel behaviors and attitudes to disabled tourists

What factors can affect the travel behaviors of people with disabilities by ages and lifestyle variable factors? When one person is disable, he/she will have different behaviors to satisfy whose needs in whose whole travelling journey. In special , the older age and younger age disable tourists who will have different travelling needs. In fact, the disabled tourists won't easy to go anywhere travelling destinations in whose whole travelling journey. So, it seems that the travelling entertainment needs won't be very much to these younger or older disabled tourists. Moreover, people with disabilities travel will be compare with people without disabilities. So, it is one key to explain why the travelling entertainment purposes or needs to disable people which are lesser than the people without disabilities.

In negative or problematic experience of travel to disabled tourists aspect, I believe that it is one travelling experiences problem is considered to need to be solved to any younger or older age disabled tourists, because they are handicapped people, they will feel walk in difficulty, even they need wheel chairs to help them to walk. So, the moving disabled problem will influence how they feel unsafe on public transport in any strange travelling countries considerable. In special, the older aged 50 and over disabled people need to catch any public transport when they need to sit on wheel chairs to go to anywhere destinations in any strange travelling countries. They will feel not convenient and unsafe when they need to sit on wheel chairs to go to anywhere destinations. These travelling places are their first time arriving places. Hence, transportation tools will be consideration problem to any disabled tourists. It seems that renting car travelling providers will be one popular or preferable choice to any younger orolder age disabled tourists. Because disabled tourists won't need to catch public transport tools, such as buses, trains, trams, taxis in unsafe, notconvenient natural travelling environment. They can drive themselves renting cars to go to anywhere travelling destinations easily or conveniently. Thus, I believe that the renting cr travelling service which is very attractive to any young or old age disabled tourist nowadays.

In general, instead of renting cars to drive behavioral change to disabled tourists usually ,renting cars behaviors which will replace to choose to catch any public transportation tools behavior to disable tourists. What kinds of other behavioral changes will impact to disabled tourists? Other aspect consideration is disabled tourist individual health problem . For example, if the disabled tourist is driving himself/herself renting cars to go to anywhere destinations in long term in the travelling country. The long distance of driving miles travelling and driving long hours spend travelling behaviors will influence the disable tourist individual nervous health to be more poor, because he/she needs to spend more time and nervous to drive whose renting car to go to anywhere in whole travelling journey. So, it is very dangerous and unsafe to the disabled tourist when he/she needs to concentrate on nervous to drive himself/herself renting car to go to anywhere destinations to travel in whose travelling journey or trip.

In consideration of the older age disabled tourist groups will be more unsafe and dangerous when he/she needs to spend much time to drive whose renting car to arrive any travelling destinations. So, it is based on this long time unsafe driving factor, the older age disabled tourist groups will choose to spend lesser time to drive to go to anywhere destinations to travel alone or with their friends and/or families in general. Similar patterns are evident in the numbers of miles travelled and the time spent to driving renting car behavior to any older age disabled tourist groups will be lesser than the younger age disabled tourist groups . Due to the long time unsave renting car self-driving feeling to the older age disabled tourists. It will impact to influence the older age disabled tourists to choose to catch any public transport or walking to replace renting car self-driving behaviors in their trips, when older age handicapped tourists loss hearing, sight, memory, recognizing physical danger, personal care difficulties disabled characteristics.

Thus, the long time renting car driving behavior which will influence the old age disabled tourists to choose to catch public transport tools to replace to rent car to drive in whose trip persuasively. So, the renting car providers will have lesser old age disable tourist number to compare to young age disabled tourist number in common. Also, the old age disable tourists will prefer to choose the travel destinations where have many public transport tools to let them to catch for their travelling journeys.

CHAPTER NINE

How social internet networking impacts traveller individual behavior

Can web site online internet networking influence traveller individual behavior changes? If web site can influence every online traveller user individual behavior change, how it influence every online user individual behavior change in order to impact his/her travelling service or arrangement change choice. For example, when the traveller walks in one travel agent's shop to find the most suitable travelling package for whose trip.

At the moment, he/she plans to find the travel agent to help him/her to arrange any travelling package. But when he/she goes back his/her home, he/she turns on his/her computer to link online travel agent website. Then, he/she discovers this online travel agent can provide more attractive travelling package similar service and he/she will compare the walk in travel agent's travelling package to this online travel agent travelling package. Although, the walk-in travelling agent can provide lesser service fee to compare this online travel agent. But , he/she feels this online travel agent can provide more attractive and enjoyable travelling entertainment and trip arrangement service to satisfy his/her travelling need. So, he/she decides to choose this online travelling agent's travelling package and it seems that the online travel agent web site can influence his/her original travelling agent target choice.

Nowadays, the most famous online development reshaping traditional marketing methods of tourism business will be possible to replace the traditional walk-in travel agent business. Because travelling consumers like to turn on computer to link to different travelling agents' websites to choose which travelling package is the cheapest or it can provide the most attractive or enjoyable entertainment arrangement in the trip. So, online travel agents will influence travelling consumers to reduce to spend time to walk in to visit any travel agent shops. The traveller prefers to spend much time to find which travelling agents' websites to find the most right online travelling agent to help him/her to arrange the trip service to replace to find the most right walk-in travelling agent at home conveniently. So, travelling agent website development can impact every traveller individual planning behavior to be changed influentially because when he/she plans to walk in to visit the identified travel agent shop, but when he/she has one desk top computer to be installed at home. Then, he/she will have another choice to buy the travelling package service. So, he/she will change his/her walk in to visit the travel agent planning behavior to change to clicking on any travel agent's website behavior.

Moreover, travelling website characteristics or attractive point is easy communication. When the traveller feels any worry or trouble, he/her need to enquire the online travelling agent immediately. He/she can send email to enquire the travelling agent to arrange travelling package similar service to walk in travel agent and he/she will compare the walk in travel agent's travelling package to this online travel agent travelling package. Although, the walk-in travelling agent can provide lesser service fee to compare this online travel agent. But, he/she feels that this online travel agent can provide more attractive and enjoyable travelling entertainment and trips service to satisfy his/her travelling need. So, he/she decides to choose this online travelling agent's travelling package and it seems that the online travel agent website can influence his/her original travelling agent target choice.

Nowadays, the most famous online development reshaping traditional marketing methods of tourism business will be possible to replace the traditional walk-in travel agent business. Because travelling walk-in consumer like to turn on computer to link to different travelling agents' websites to choose which travelling package is the cheapest or it can provide the most attractive or enjoyable entertainment arrangement .

Thus, online travelling information search tool can attract travellers to choose to find any travel agents' websites from internet to replace walk-in travel agents' shops influentially. Also, it seems online travelling service will be popular to replace walk-in travelling service in possible.

- Cultural distance on satisfaction and respect travel intention

Every country cultural difference is different. How and why cultural difference has a real impact on tourist satisfaction and it can also influence to repeat travel. Is cultural tourism one major factor to influence tourist to repeat travelling intention or choice to the country in international tourism choice market? For example, China and India have similar culture. Their cultural difference is not much, e.g. eating cultural habit is similar , entertainment cultural habit is similar. These both countries people do not want to spend much money in eating and entertainment both aspects. Hence, these two countries people do not consider how to consume to enjoy entertainment and eat expensive food. Hence, it is based on cultural similar reason. These both countries tourists will prefer to choose to repeat travelling either China or India. When the Indian tourists had chosen to go to China to travel in the first time. Then, the Indian tourists will choose to go to China to travel in second time again. Also, the Indian tourists had chosen to go to China to travel in first time. Then, the Chinese tourists will choose to go to India to travel in second time again.

What factors influence China and India touists repect to travel between these both countries. The factors will include cheap air ticket price, cheap hotel living price , less economic cost factor. However, I believe the similar cultural factor will be the major factor to influence many Chinese and Indian tourist prefer to choose to repeat travelling between these both countries.

As my indication to these both countries people have similar eating habits, choosing foods, low health foods, common foods choice eating at cheap restaurant habitual consumption. Also, they have similar entertainment habits, their entertainment demad is not high. They like to ride bicycles to go to anywhere to travel. They like to go to swim, play backetball, football etc. sports. These all sports are cheap sport consumption. So, it based on similar individual low enjoyment demand and low health, food quality demand similar cultural factors. Chinese and Indian people have no long distance cultural difference between eating and entertainment habitual factor will include them to choose to repeact travelling between these both countries. Due to China and India have many restaurants can provide cheap food or sport service providers can provide diffent kinds of cheap sport entertainment consumption to satisfy their cheap food and cheap entertainment needs in their journey in China or India anywhere. So, it explains that why these both countries tourists will repeat to travel these both countries again after they had visited China or India to travel in first time. So, the similar cultural factor can impact these both countries tourists to repeat to go to these both countries to travel again. Hence, if these two countries' cultural distance is far or different, then themselves countries' tourists won't choose to repeat travel between themselves when these two countries for cultural distance toutists had visited to another country in first time. Hence, culture has been continuously considered as a much factor which tourists consider in terms of choice of the destination travelling place. Also, it explains cultural distance which can make tourist individual has less satisfaction to concern to tourists to repeat travels.

Otherwise, for far cultural distance two countries case example, such as Chinese and American , these two countries people's eating habit and entertainment cultural needs are different. For eating habit difference example, American like to eat poks, beefs, chickens, potatos to replace rice and other foods. Otherwise, Chinese like to wat rice, vegatables more than potatoes, porks , beefs for lunch , dinner . So , their eating habits are very different. Also, American like to drive boats on the seasor drive crs to go to anywhere to travel on holidays for sports or holiday entertainment activities . Otherwise, Chinese like to play backetball, football, ride bicycle of cheaper sport entertainment on holidays. So, American entertainment activities are more expensive to compare Chinese. Also, US and China , like families whose power distance is dfferent, such as every per family powerful member is parents, who have more power to give opinions to choose anywhere to travel for whose sons and/or daughters whole famililY members travelling arrangement.

Therefore, if the Us family powerful members, such as at least one son or/ and ond daughter members who need t choose to go to which country to travel if the family powerful members, such as the child/ children's parent feel China's food taste or entertainment activities are totally different to be similar to their country's food taste and entertainment activities habitually after their whole fmily members had travelled to China in first time before. Although, their son(s) and daughter(s) will hope to go to China to repect travel again. But, due to the US family parents are their son(s) and daughter(S) powerful decider to make any travelling decision to choose which country will be next time travelling destination. If their parents feel China's eating and entertainment culture is totally different to their countries. Then, the US family will not choose to repeat travel to the China country again any more easily, beause this US family can not feel satisfactory when they visited China in their first time before, due to they feel China 's food and entertainment cultures are totally different to their US country. So, the cultural distance factor will influence the US family don't choose China to fo repeat travel again.

Consequently, different countries' similar or different cultural factor will influence the country's tourists choose to repeact travel to the country again. So, any country needs to know what its culture is in order to attract the similar cultural countries tourists to repeat travel to itself country more easily.

CHAPTER TEN

Lifestyle factor influences travel behavior

Whether do different countries tourists‘ different lifestyle which can influence their travel consumption behaviors? Even, which countries that they will choose to go to travel. For example, when one tourist who owns himself/herself often to drive to go to anywhere habitually. The tourist's driving car habital behavior which will influence that he /she will feel need to rent car to travel to anywhere habitually , when he/she selects to go to the country to travel. Hence, if he/she feels the tourism destination has no any rent car service providers to provide him/her to rent any car to travel anywhere in the country's travel destination. Does the country lack rent car service factor which will influence that he/she will still choose to go to the country to travel in preference? For example, when one New Zealander's family who own at least one car at home. So, the New Zealand whole family every member can often drive car to go to anywhere , even, one family member had driven one car to leave his/her home. So, driving own car activity or behavior has been one habitual activity to influence the New Zealand every member to feel the travelling destination needs have rent car service provider supplies cars to let them to rent to travel. The driving car lifestyle has caused the whole New Zealander family driving habit. When the family's sons) and/or daughter(s) need(s) to go to school or go to shopping as well as their parents also need to drive their cars to go to office to work in themselves home town often. In common, there are many New Zealanders who will have at least one car at home because they feel that they can drive their themselves cars to go to anywhere in New Zealand more than waiting bus or tram or train or ferry etc. public transportation tools more conveniently. So, New Zealanders' driving own car habit will influence their lifestyle to feel that they also need to rent cars to travel to go to any where to travel to replace to wait public transportation tools choice in the travelling destination during their journey.

For shopping trips is more influenced by their driving car activities. So, it seems that this New Zealander families will be influenced to their tourism destination need, they need the tourism destination has car renting service provider to be supplied anywhere to let them can drive the renting cars to go to anywhere in tourism destination. It means that when the tourim destination has less rent car providers can provide renting car services to drive anywhere or it has none any renting car service providers are existing in the tourism destination. Then, the renting car service providers number shortage or none any renting car service providers to be provided to the country's tourism destination, which will cause the New Zealander families do not perfer to choose to go to the country to travel generally, e.g. Hong Kong, China, Korea these Asia countries have no many rent car service providers in these countries. So, the New Zealand families won't prefer to choose to go these countries to travel when they discover these Asia countries lack enough rent car service providers to let them to drive to travel in themselves conveniently. Otherwise, America, England, Japan etc. countries have many rent car service providers. So, these countries will be this New Zealander families' preferable tourism countries. Thus, the New Zealand families' driving ownership car lifestyle will influence their travel behaviors to choose to go to the country which can have many rent car providers in the tourism country any where tourism destinations in preference.

Thus, whether the country has renting car service providers , it will be variable factor to influence any country's car ownship families' driving car travel behaviors in their journey in order to let they feel that they can drive themselves ownship cars to go to anywhere to travel conveniently, even when they leave their countries. Hence, these countries' car ownship driving habitual families' behaviors will be influenced their tourism destination or location decision choice when the country has many renting car service providers in preference as well as this renting car service provider supplying factor will be more important to influence the habitual driving own car traveller to be preferable choice to compare other factors, e.g. cheap entertainment consumption providers factor which include cheap hotel living fee, cheap food price consumption etc. expenditure in the travelling country.

Thur, it explains that different countries' car ownship tourists , whose driving own car activities will cause their daily lifestyles, then their daily driving own car lifestyles will influence their tourism destination choices indirectly. So, it seems that lifestyle can be a outcome variable (or dependent variable) factor to influence travel behavior in any travelling built environment. The travelling built environment characteristics can include density measures (population density, job density), job-housing density). These travelling buit environment factor can repreent what the city resident's lifestyle. For example, where the location in relation to local centre or regional centre to the country's residents are living. This country resident's living location will cause this country resident's lifestyles , e.g. holiday or leisure whether it is low budget, active and adventurous or frequent traveller with second place or self-orgnized , family oriented or close to home and unadventurour. Hence, the country's living built environment will influence the country's resident's lifestyles. Due to different countries' residents will have different lifestyles. Hence, built environments and lifestlyes have relationship to influence every country's residents when they need to go to other countries to travel in their holidays. For example, frequent travellers are usually living in big and busy cities, otherwise, non -frequent travellers are ususally living in the countrysides, where there are less offices or factories are built to let people to work. So, big city will bring busy feeling to the country's residents, then they will be influenced to feel need to often to go to travel for leisure intention in their holidays. Otherwise, countryside will bring not busy or quiet environment feeling to the country's residents, then they won't feel working feeling when they are living in counryside. So, they won't feel need to go t o anywhere to travel in their holidays often.

Hence, built environment will bring either busy or not busy (quiet environment feeing) to the both different country residents when they are living in the places. Their living places will cause their lifestyles are different. Then, they will be influences to feel have more frequent travelling needs or less frequent travelling needs to explain why every country people will have more or less frequent travelling needs.

● How any why peer-to-peer
accommodation can impact
business tourism pattern

I shall explain how any why peer-to-peer accomodation can attract business tourisms to choose business tourism intention? Usually , employees or employers buy business trips, why they choose one particular travelling company over another and why the business tourists choose to travel when the peer (more than one buiness tourists) who will choose to peer-to-per accommodation business tourism pattern more than the more expensive hotel living comfortable feeling business tourism pattern.

Business travel agents need to know or understand what reasons the employer or employee feels peer-to-peer accommodation business tourism motivation is more suitable or better to compare hotel living comfortable feeling business tourism pattern. Why can business tourism accommodation choice factor influence the business tourist's business trip choice.

Business trip means work related travel to an irregular place or work and it represents that one employee or more than on employees business tourists whose expenses are paid by the business ,he or she or they work(s) for. So, in employer's business trip expense view point, he/she expects the employee or employees can choose the most cheap expenses for whose business trip. It also means that the exployer does not expect that it is a high quality journey for the employee's or employees' business trip. The business tourism is year-round, peaking in spring and autumn , but still with high levels of activity in the summer and winter months. It may be long time ot short time, e.g. less than one month or more than one month, evern more than half year for the business trip. When the employee is employees are working permanent full time employment. It is not for leisure intention, it means that the employer does not hope employee or employees spend(s) extra more expense to spend any leisure or goes (go) to any destinations to visit in their/her/his whole business trip.

Hence, it is based on the cheap expenses for the business trip aim, employer usually demands employees or employees to choose the peer-to-peer be cheaper accommodation to live or the employer will help its employee(s) to choose the peer-to-peer cheaper accommodation to live. So, it seems that expensive hotel living facilities won't be the preferable accommodation choice for employer because the business trip pay or reimburse the employee. Hence, business travel agencies ought not help the business tourists to choose expensive travel package, e.g. expensive hotel accommodation on the trip, expensive transportation tools, e.g. taxi renting service to get to buisness meetings, the cheapt peer-to-peer cheap hostel accommodation and cheap transportation tool, e.g. travel buses pre-booking service, or cheap restaurant choice vacation incentives package is more attractive to let them/him/her to choose for their/her/his business trip.

A business person or a peer-to-peer business people also have /her expect to take advantage of frequent flyer schemes which allow him/her/them to take leisure trip with airlines when they/he/she is /are accumulated sufficient miles in the chep or tair ticket(s) to catch air plane for businss trip. Hence, he/she /they expect(s) to earn airlines expenses from whose frequent flyer schemes when they/he/she can claim to original air ticket price from whose employer, but in fact, peer-to-peer business tourists or individual business tourist pay lesser ait ticket charge from whose frequent flying program accumulated sufficient miles, even no any payment. So, airlines can benefit the business traveller, such as improved in competition milages programs, quick check in and online check in, lounges with broadband connection etc. service.

Why does peer-to-oeer accommodation living factor is the most influential to any business tourist(s) to choose the travel agent? In employer's business trip expensive view point, if it has many employees need to go to other countries business trips for long days frequently. Then, the employer will consider whether the every day accommodation living cost is expensive or not. So, comparison hotel and peer-to-peer hostle price, hotel accommodation price is usually higher than hostle accommodation rent price. When peer-to-peer accommodation has been shown to positively impact to business trip employers in popular. Because any business spending will be one important considerable factor to influence employers to choose. However, the accommodation renting price will be more influential to impact business tourism cost. Hence, employers will estimate every whole business trip expenses how it can impact peer-to-peer or hotel accommodation choice. So, the living budget factor will be one important influential factor to influence any employers how to choose where are the suitable destination for every individual business tourist or peer-to-peer group business tourists to live. So, it seems small size peer-to-peer hostles are compared to large size expensive hotels more suitable for business tourists.

Although, it is possible that individual employee or a group peer-to-peer employees will feel peer-to-peer hostle is not more safe than hotel accommodation. But, their/his/her employer usually does not consider safety, comfortable environment issue for their/his/her every business trip. They only consider loe accommodation price issue. So, the accommodation choice will be one critical factor to influence employers how to help their individual employee or a group peer-to-peer employees to choose where he/she/they will live when he/she/they arrive(s) the destination for whose every business trip. Hence, it seems that accommodation will be one critical factor to influence anywhere to be chosen to live for any business trips to their individual employee or group peer-to-peer employees‘ needs.

● Factors influence local tourists' destination choice

What are the main internal and external factors to influence local tourist's domestic travelling choice behaviors and detination choice decision making? What are the social , cultural , personal psychological factors to influence the decision-making of local tourists to travel to different types of tourism destinations in domestic travelling destinations, e.g. attractions, available amenities, accessinility, image price external factors. They can influence local tourist's destination choice behaviors. Does the individual occupational reason can influence local tourist's local destination travelling choice? So, any travel agents need to develop and promote of domestic destination need to determine the factors influencing tourist's destination choice.

In a local destination tourist individual productive way, how loca tourism agents can bring what factors to influence or charge whose local destination travelling behavioral changes. For example, tourist individual behavior and destination choice factor, the comparision between the current local tourism destinations choice and the past local tourism destinations choice factor. Instead of local different travelling destination prices comparison, journeys comparison . What are the other internal and external factor to influence the local tourist's travelling destinations choices behaviors, e.g. attending local festivals, events, taste local cuisine and be part of unique features of a destination. These will be valuable external or internal factors to influence the local tourist's local destinatons choices. So, different countries‘ local travelling destinations will need have a number og key elements that attract visitors and meet their needs. The key elements may include , for example, primary activities, physical setting and social / cultural attributes primary external activities elements, and secondary elements may include catering and shopping, and addition elements/ accessibility and tourists information providing to local tourists.

Due to local destinaton tourism must be cheaper than overseas or foreigh destination tourism. So, the local torust travel agents need to provide thei travelling services to local tourists, more attractions, accessibility , amenities, excellent available packages activities and ancillary services to compare overseas tourism destinations. Because the local tourists will compare the overseas different destinations travelling places to decide whether they ought choose to travel overseas or local different destinations at the moment. So, any entertainment activities concern local destinations which will be local tourists' perferable comparative travelling services to the local travel agent and the overseas travelling service in order to decide whether he/she ought choose local travelling or overseas travelling at the moment.

Hence, local different travelling destinatons attractive factor will be one important influential factor to influence local tourist's travelling choices. However, a tourist's attitude, decisions, activities, ideas or travelling experiences evaluating and searching of any tourism service behaviors will influence the final travelling destinaton choice decision whether he/she ought choose to go to overseas or local travel. He/she will consider how to spend time and money and effort to carry on any kinds of entertainment activitied in whose local or overseas journeys. So, the different destination local and overseas internal travelling price and spending entertainment time in journey and spending effort to arranging every travelling entertainment which every will be one considerable issue to compare budget to overseas and local different travelling destinations. If the tourist feel whose country , e.g. American's local travelling destination budget is spend less than overseas travelling destination too much. Then, the American will choose to local travelling destinations more than overseas travelling destinations and the moment. So, travelling budget will one factor to influence the tourist to choose whether overseas or local travelling.

So, it seems that time, money and effort will be another factor to influence the tourist will be another factor to influence the tourist chooses to go to overseas or local travelling destinations, instead of different travelling entertainment provider choices factor in the local or overseas travelling destinations . Moreover, the tourist's indvidual income, the local and overseas living condition, formation of cultural and aesthetic tasts, price of local and overseas travelling service and discounts, loca and overseas travelling destinations' temperature or weather viable, e.g. number of sunny days, geographical condition, cultural and natural resource, medical tourism etc. external factors will influence the tourist individual final travelling decision to choose either local tourism or overseas tourism entertainment decision.

CHAPTER ELEVEN

Tourist individual driving behavior how to impact travel behavior

Does every tourist individual driving behavior influence whose travel behavioral choice? However, individual mobility decisions are possible difficulties for measures aiming at tourist individual travelling behavioral changes and links them to the transport need aspect when the tourist arrivee the destination to travel. For example, whether the travelling destination has bus public transportation tool supplies or ferry transportation tool supplies or taxi transportation tool supplied ot train or tram etc. different public transportation tools to influence the tourist individual travelling destination choice.

When every country decides to develop travel industry. It needs to understand how to arrange what kind of public transportation tools to be supplied to satisfy any countries' tourists mobility needs in whose journeys in order to achieve tourism planning for public transportation system to attract different countries' tourists to choose to arrive itself different destinations to travel more easily. So, the country's transportation services supplies will have permanently impacted to every tourist individual travel behavior towards more mobility when he/she arrives to the country to travel.

Can transportation system factor influence tourist individual travelling desination decision? it depends on the tourist individual attitude or transport needs of decisions. For example, if the city , e.g. New York has many tourists, who are high income, young gender, high education level tourists. Then, they will choose more expensive and comforable train more than cheap and not comfortable bus transportation tool. So, I assume that

the year has many high income, high education , high social class occupation tourists arrive US , New York city . Then, they will choose train more than bus transportation tool to go to anywhere to travel in New York city. So, it is not represent that the city has many cheaper public transportation tool, such as many buses number to be supplied , the bus public public transporation tool can bring more income to attract overseas tourists to come to New York travel. It depends on whether the tourist individual characteristics, e.g. high or low income, more or less comfortable transportion tool supplies needs or high or low educational level, alone tourist or family tourist or friend relationship tourist. Any one of these tourist individul psychological factors will influence the tourist to choose either cheap and less comfortable public tool system or expensive and more comfortable public tool system to be supplied to the city to travel. So, the city's comfortable or not comfortable public transportation tool supplies which will influence the overseas tourists how to choose the city to travel.
However, on the tourist's habitual behavior of catching which kind of transportation tools, this factor will bring to influence how to choose the kind of transportation tool(s) whether the city can provide choice to let the overseas tourist to make where travelling decision when he/she arrives to the coutry. However, his/her transporatin tool catching habit will be possible to influenc whose travel times for public transport use, instead of which kind of transport tool(s) he/she will choose to catch when he/she arrives the country to travel.
In conclusion, the tourist's age, income, occupation, education level will influence how the tourist's transportation choice in himself/herself country, then it also bring this question: will influence the tourist individual destination choice if the country can provide or can not provide the kind of public transportation tool(s) to let the tourist to choose to catch in his/her journey in the country's city. Hence, it explains that why every country's pubic transporation tool supplies will influence the tourist to choose where to travel in the country.

11.1 What are usually travel behaviors and attitudes to disabled tourists

What factors can affect the travel behaviors of people with disabilites by ages and lifestyle variable factors? When one person is disable, he/she will have different behaviors to satisfy whose needs in whose whole travelling journey. In special , the older age and younger age disable tourists who will have diffeent travelling needs. In fact, the disabled tourists won't easy to go anywhere travelling destinations in whose whole travelling journey. So, it seems that the travelling entertainment needs won't be very much to these younger or older disabled tourists. Moreover, people with disabilities travel will be compare with people without disabilities. So, it is one key to explain why the travelling entertainment purposes or needs to disable people which are lesser than the people without disabilities.

In negative or problematic experience of travel to disabled tourists aspect, I believe that it is one travelling expereinces problem is considered to need to be solved to any younger or older age disabled tourists, because they are handicapped people, they will feel walk in difficulty, even they need wheelchaires to help them to walk. So, the visiable mving disabled problem will influence how they feel unsafe on public transport in any strange travelling countries considerabllly. In special, the older aged 50 and over disabled people need to catch any public transport when they need to sit on wheelchaires to go to anywhere destinations in any strange travelling countries. They will feel unconvenient and unsafe when they need to sit on wheelchaires to go to anywhere destinations. These travelling places are their first time arriving places. Hence, transportation tools will be consideration problem to any disabled tourists. It seems that renting car travelling providers will be one popular or preferable choice to any younger orolder age disabled tourists. Because disabled tourists won't need to catch public transport tools, such as buses, trains, trams, taxis in unsafe, unconvenient natural travelling environment. They can drive themselves renting cars to go to anywhere travelling destinations easily or conveniently. Thus, I believe that the renting cr travelling service which is very attractive to any young or old age disabled tourist nowadays.

In general, instead of renting cars to drive behavioral change to disabled tourists usually ,renting cars behaviors which will replace to choose to catch any public transportation tools behavior to disable tourists. What kinds of other behavioral changes will impact to disabled tourists? Other aspect consideration is disabled tourist individual health problem . For example, if the disabled tourist is driving himself/herself renting cars to go to anywhere destinations in long term in the travelling country. The long distance of driving miles travelling and driving long hours spend travelling behaviors will influence the disable tourist individual nervous health to be more poor, because he/she needs to spend more time and nervous to drive whose renting car to go to anywhere in whole travelling journey. So, it is very dangerous and unsafe to the disabled tourist when he/she needs to concentrate on nervous to drive himself/herself renting car to go to anywhere destinations to travel in whose travelling journey or trip.

In consideration of the older age disabled tourist groups will be mor unsafe and dangerous when he/she needs to spend much time to drive whose renting car to arrive any travelling destinations. So, it is based on this long time unsafe driving factor, the older age disabled tourit groups will choose to spend lesser time to drive to go to anywhere destinations to travel alone or with their friends and/or families in general. Similar patterns are evident in the numbers of miles travelled and the time spent to driving renting car behavior to any older age disabled tourist groups will be lesser than the younger age disabled tourist groups . Due to the long time unsae renting car self-driving feeling to the older age disabled tourists. It will impact to influence the older age disabled tourists to choose to catch any public transport or walking to replace renting car self-driving behaviors in their trips, when older age handicapped tourists loss hearing, sight, memory, recognizing physical danger, personal care difficulties disabled characteristics.

Thus, the long time renting car driving behavior which will influence the old age disabled tourists to choose to catch public transport tools to replace to rent car to drive in whose trip persuasively. So, the renting car providers will have lesser old age disable tourist number to compare to young age disabled tourist number in common. Also, the old age disable touristss will prefer to choose the travel destinations where have many public transport tools to let them to catch for their travelling journeys.

11.2 How social internet networking impacts traveller individual behavior

Can web site online internet networking influence traveller individual behavior changes? If web site can influence every online traveller user individual behavior change, how it influence every online user individual behavior change in order to impact his/her travelling service or arrangement change choice. For example, when the traveller walks in one travel agent's shop to find the most suitable travelling packge for whose trip. At the moment, he/she pland to find the travel agent to help him/her to arrange any travelling package. But when he/she goes back his/her home, he/she turns on his/her computer to link online travel agent website. Then, he/she discovers this online travel agent can provide more attractive travelling package similar service ans he/she will compare the walk in travel agent's travelling package to this online travel agent travelling package. Although, the walk-in travelling agent can provide lesser service fee to compare this online travel agent. But , he/she feels this online travel agent can provide more attractive and enjoyable travelling entertainment and trip arrangement service to satisfy his/her travelling need. So, he/she decides to choose this online travelling agent's travelling package and it seems that the online travel agent web site can influence his/her original travelling agent targe choice.

Nowadays, the most famous online developmet reshaping traditional marketing methods of tourism business will be possible to replace the traditional walk-in travel agent business. Because travelling consumers like to turn on computer to link to different travelling agents' websites to choose which travelling package is the cheapest or it can provie the most attractive or enjoyable entertainment arrangement in the trip. So, online travel agents will influence travelling consumers to reduce to spend time to walk in to visit any travel agent shops. The traveller prefers to spend much time to find which travelling agents' websites to find the most right online travelling agent to help him/her to arrange the trip service to replace to find the most right walk-in travelling agent at home conveniently. So, travelling agent website development can impact every traveller individual planning behavior to be changed influentially because when he/she plans to walk in to visit the identified travel agent shop, but when he/she has one desk top computer to be installed at home. Then, he/she will have another choice to buy the travelling package service. So, he/she will change his/her walk in to visit the travel agent planning behavior to change to clicking on any travel agent's website behavior.

Moreover, travelling website characteristics or attractive point is easy communication. When the traveller feels any worry or trouble, he/her need to enquire the online travelling agent immediately. He/she can send email to enquire the travelling agent to arrange travelling package similar service to walk in travel agent and he/she will compare the walk in travel agent's travelling package to this online travel agent travelling package. Although, the walk-in travelling agent can provide lesser service fee to compare this online travel agent. But, he/she feels that this online travel agent can provide more attractive and enjoyable travelling entertainment and trips service to satisfy his/her travelling need. So, he/she decides to choose this online travelling agent's travelling package and it seems that the online travel agent website can influence his/her original travelling agent target choice.

Nowadays, the most famous online development reshaping traditional marketing methods of tourism business will be possible to replace the traditional walk-in travel agent business. Because travelling walk-in consumer like to turn on computer to link to different travelling agents' websites to choose which travelling package is the cheapest or it can provide the most attractive or enjoyable entertainment arrangement .

Thus, online travelling information search tool can attract travellers to choose to find any travel agents' websites from internet to replace walk-in travel agents' shopes influentially. Also, it seems online travelling service will be popular to replace walk-in travelling service in possible.

9 798885 695893

Printed by Libri Plureos GmbH in Hamburg, Germany